DALESMAN PUBLISHING COMPANY LTD.,
CLAPHAM, VIA LANCASTER
North Yorkshire
First published 1980
Second edition 1983
Reprinted 1986
© presentation, Dalesman Publishing Company Ltd., 1980, 1986
ISBN: 0 85206 708 9

CHARLOTTE BRONTË

Printed by Howe Brothers Limited, Swan Street, Gateshead, Tyne and Wear.
Telephone: (091) 477 1091

2

# The Brontës

## An Illustrated
## Selection of
## Prose and Poetry

DALESMAN BOOKS
1986

FARM WALLS AT STANBURY

# Contents

The diaeresis has been omitted from the name Bronte in the body of the book.

## Illustrations

SIMON WARNER: pages 1, 3, 7, 11, 12, 22, 27, 37, 40, 49, 50, 55, 88, 91, 92. HAWORTH PARSONAGE: 2, 14, 17, 18, 20, 45, 58, 77, 83. CLIFFORD ROBINSON: 4, 28, 30, 43, 52, 54, 56, 61, 81, 96 and outside back cover. YORKSHIRE TELEVISION: Study of Brontë family, from the successful television series by Christopher Fry. W. R. MITCHELL: 9, 25, 47, 63, 64, 66, 69, 70, 84, 87, 95. P. WALSHAW: 34. RUSSELL FIRTH: 51. BOB COLLINS: 53. DEREK WIDDICOMBE: 73. Wm. FARNSWORTH: 74.

# An Introduction

WE SEEM TO KNOW a great deal about the Brontes, but they remain strange, mysterious, enigmatic. The Bronte sisters, though weak and consumptive, poured out their souls in a stream of literary works. Even today, after much research and speculation, we can only guess at the well-springs of their inspiration, yet it is in those works that their characters are most surely revealed.

In this anthology, the Brontes speak for themselves. They who were capable of such intense and sustained writing do not really deserve to have their work fragmented; my selection may stimulate some who have so far read only the Bronte life story, to scan their novels and poems. What appears in this book is at least wholly theirs –undiluted Bronte, without the intercession of critic or biographer. It is a small selection, and they wrote copiously.

There was much sadness in their lives. The Rev. Patrick Bronte, who arrived at Haworth so hopefully in 1820, buried a wife and all six children within the space of 34 years. The Bronte children kept their spirits intact through a long-cultivated capacity to switch off thoughts of the generally dreary world in which they lived, to dwell in a colourful, fascinating world of fantasy. This feverishly talented family often knew elation and joy, and it was to some of the more joyful of their writings that I was drawn.

The facts about their life at Haworth are well-known through a host of other books. Haworth, their home, lies on a spur of the Southern Pennines. From the front windows of their home at the Parsonage they saw a well-filled graveyard, reminding them of the brevity of human life, and a church witnessing, with full Victorian certainty, to

Opposite: Main Street, Haworth

the better life, which lay beyond the grave. With an Irish father, and Cornish mother, the children were almost certain to be mentally agile, richly imaginative. With their mother dead, and a well-meaning but rather austere aunt presiding over the parsonage, the children were thrown back on their own considerable resources.

Haworth was an industrious village, yet at the back door of the parsonage began the moor – a gritstone moor, briefly spectacular when the ling showed its purple flowers, and whitened in the boggy places by the tufty heads of cotton grass. The moor coloured their lives; they knew it at all seasons of the year, rejoicing in the interplay of sunshine and storm.

Emily, obsessed by the elemental forces which created and shaped the moor, transformed those forces into human passions through her story "Wuthering Heights." Charlotte also loved the wilderness. but less intensely than Emily; she wove romantic stories about it. Then there was Anne – sweet, sensitive, pious Anne – and, bringing moments of almost savage intensity into the family life, Branwell Bronte, a frustrated genius.

In the year 1847, three Bronte novels were published, and in due course they gripped Victorian England. Charlotte's "Jane Eyre," Emily's "Wuthering Heights" and Anne's "Agnes Grey" were so unlike other books. Only Charlotte's work immediately commended itself to the reading public, but soon Emily's story of unbridled passions was seen to be something quite exceptional. It continues to haunt us.

The Brontes have been a part of my life since childhood. My maternal great-grandfather was a personal friend of Patrick Bronte; my paternal grandfather was writing about this remarkable family early this century. There has thus been a special pleasure in selecting extracts from their works. There is, of course, no real substitute for reading the works themselves . . .

W. R. MITCHELL

TOP WITHENS

# Call of the Moors

For the moors! For the moors! where the short grass
Like velvet beneath us should lie!
For the moors! For the moors! where the high pass
Rose sunny against the clear sky!

For the moors! where the linnet was trilling
Its song on the old granite stone,
Where the lark, the wild skylark, was filling
Every breast with delight like its own.

EMILY BRONTE

My sister Emily had a particular love for (the moors), and there is not a knoll of heather, not a branch of fern, not a young bilberry leaf, not a fluttering lark or linnet, but reminds me of her. The distant prospects were Anne's delight, and when I look round, she is in the blue tints, the pale mists, the waves and shadows of the horizon. In the hill-country silence, their poetry comes by lines and stanzas into my mind.

CHARLOTTE BRONTE
*Writing about her dead sisters, May, 1850.*

This is certainly a beautiful country. In all England, I do not believe that I could have fixed on a situation so completely removed from the stir of society.

EMILY BRONTE
*An observation by Mr. Lockwood in "Wuthering Heights".*

Wuthering Heights was hewn in a wild workshop, with simple tools, out of homely materials. The statuary found a granite block on a solitary moor: gazing thereon, he saw how from the crag might be elicited a head, savage, swart, sinister; a form moulded with at least one element of grandeur – power. He wrought with a crude chisel, and from no model but the vision of his meditations. With time and labour, the crag took human shape; and there it stands colossal, dark, and frowning, half statue, half rock: in the former sense, terrible and goblin-like; in the latter, almost beautiful, for its colouring is of mellow grey, and moorland moss clothes it; and heath, with its blooming bells and balmy fragrance, grows faithfully close to the giant's foot.

CHARLOTTE BRONTE
*Preface to the 1850 edition of Emily's "Wuthering Heights".*

High waving heather, 'neath stormy blasts bending,
Midnight and moonlight and bright shining stars;
Darkness and glory rejoicingly blending,
Earth rising to heaven and heaven descending,
Man's spirit away from its drear dungeon sending.
Bursting the fetters and breaking the bars.

But lovelier than corn-fields all waving
in emerald and scarlet and gold
Are the slopes where the north-wind is raving,
And the glens where I wandered of old —

EMILY BRONTE

My favourite seat was a smooth and broad stone, rising white and dry from the very middle of the beck, and only to be got at by wading through the water, a feat I accomplished barefoot.

CHARLOTTE BRONTE
*Describing "The Bronte Waterfall".*

Come to Haworth as soon as you can; the heath is in bloom now; I have waited and watched for its purple signal as the forerunner of your coming. It will not be quite faded before the 16th, but after that it will soon grow sere.

CHARLOTTE BRONTE
*Writing to Mrs. Gaskell, September, 1853.*

A Heaven so clear, an earth so calm,
So sweet, so soft, so hushed an air,
And deepening still the dream-like charm
Wild moor-sheep feeding everywhere.

That was the scene, I knew it well;
I knew the turfy pathway's sweep,
That, winding o'er each billowing swell,
 Marked out the tracks of wandering sheep.

EMILY BRONTE

"Nature is now at her evening prayers: she is kneeling before those red hills. I see her prostrate on the great steps of her altar, praying for a fair night for mariners at sea, for travellers in deserts, for lambs on moors, and unfledged birds in woods. Caroline, I see her! and I will tell you what she is like: she is like what Eve was when she and Adam stood alone on earth . . . I saw – I now see – a woman-Titan: her robe of blue air spreads to the outskirts of the heather, where yonder flock is grazing; a veil white as an avalanche sweeps from her head to her feet, and arabesques of lightning, flame on its borders. Under her breast, I see her zone, purple like that horizon: through its blush shines the star of the evening. Her steady eyes I cannot picture; they are clear – they are deep as lakes – they are lifted and full of worship – they tremble with the softness of love and the lustre of prayer. Her forehead has the expanse of a cloud, and is paler than the early moon, risen long before dark, gathers: she reclines her bosom on the ridge of Stillbro' Moor; her mighty hands are joined beneath it . . . I will stay out here with my mother Eve, in these days called Nature. I love her – undying, mighty being! Heaven may have faded from her brow when she fell in paradise; but all that is glorious on earth shines there still."

CHARLOTTE BRONTE
*From "Shirley".*

The abrupt descent of Peniston Crags particularly attracted her notice, especially when the setting sun shone on it and the topmost heights, and the whole extent of landscape besides, lay in shadow. I explained that they were bare masses of stone, with hardly enough earth in their clefts to nourish a stunted tree. "And why are they bright so long after it is evening here?" she pursued. "Because they are a great deal higher up than we are," replied I; "you could not climb them – they are too high and steep. In winter the frost is always there before it comes to us; and deep into summer I have found snow under that black hollow on the north-east side."

EMILY BRONTE
*From "Wuthering Heights"*

Well, well, the sad minutes are moving
Though loaded with trouble and pain;
And sometime the loved and the loving
Shall meet on the mountains again.

EMILY BRONTE

"Let us rest here," said St. John, as we reached the first stragglers of a battalion of rocks, guarding a sort of pass, beyond which the beck rushed down a waterfall; and where, still a little further, the mountain shook off turf and flower, had only heath for raiment, and crag for gem – where it exaggerated the wild to the savage, and exchanged the fresh for the frowning – where it guarded the forlorn hope of solitude, and a last refuge for silence.

CHARLOTTE BRONTE
*From "Jane Eyre"*

There shines the moon, at noon of night –
Vision of glory – Dream of light!
Holy as heaven – undimmed and pure,
Looking down on the lonely moor –
And lonelier still beneath her ray
That drear moor stretches far away.
Till it seems strange that aught can lie
Beyond its zone of silver sky.

EMILY BRONTE
*Written when she was 18 years old.*

The snow is quite gone here, and I can only see two white spots on the whole range of moors; the sky is blue and the larks are singing, and the becks are all brim full . . . The air blows so sweetly.

EMILY BRONTE
*From "Wuthering Heights."*

HAWORTH OLD RECTORY.

# Life at Home

My home is humble and unattractive to strangers, but to me it contains what I shall find nowhere else in the world – the profound, and intense affection which brothers and sisters feel for each other when their minds are cast in the same mould, their ideas drawn from the same source – when they have clung to each other from childhood, and when disputes have never sprung up to divide them.

CHARLOTTE BRONTE

It is past twelve o'clock Anne and I have not tidied ourselves, done our bed work, or done our lessons and we want to go out

14

to play. We are going to have for dinner Boiled Beef, Turnips, potatoes and apple pudding. The kitchin is in a very untidy state Anne and I have not done our music exercise which consists of *b major* Tabby said on my putting a pen in her face Ya pitter pottering there instead of pilling a potate. I answered O Dear, O Dear, O Dear I will directly with that I get up, take a knife and begin pilling . . .

EMILY AND ANNE BRONTE
*Writing light-heartedly in the Haworth Parsonage kitchen.*

I should like uncommonly to be in the dining-room at home, or in the kitchen, or in the back kitchen. I should like even to be cutting up the hash, with the clerk and some register people at the other table, and you standing by, watching that I put enough flour, and not too much pepper, and above all, that I save the best pieces of the leg of mutton for Tiger and Keeper, the first of which personages would be jumping about the dish and carving knife, and the latter standing like a devouring flame on the kitchen floor. To complete the picture, Tabby blowing the fire, in order to boil the potatoes to a sort of vegetable glue! How divine are these recollections to me at this moment! Yet I have no thought of coming home just now. I lack a real pretext for doing so; it is true this place is dismal to me, but I cannot go home without a fixed prospect when I get there; and this prospect must not be a situation; that would be jumping out of the frying-pan into the fire.

CHARLOTTE BRONTE
*In a letter from Brussels to Emily at Haworth, 1843.*

Anne and I should have picked the black currants if it had been fine and sunshiny. I must hurry off now to my turning and ironing. I have plenty of work on hand, and writing, and am altogether full of business.

EMILY BRONTE
*From her Diary, July 30, 1845.*

Charlotte has lately been to Hathersage, in Derbyshire, on a visit of three weeks to Ellen Nussey. She is now sitting sewing in the dining-room. Emily is ironing upstairs. I am sitting in the dining-room in the rocking chair before the fire with my feet on the fender. Papa is in the parlour. Tabby and Martha are, I think, in the kitchen. Keeper and Flossy are, I do not know where. Little Dick is hopping in his cage.

ANNE BRONTE
*From her Diary, July 31, 1845.*

I smelt the rich scent of the heating spices; and admired the shining kitchen utensils, the polished clock, decked with holly, the silver mugs ranged on a tray ready to be filled with mulled ale for supper; and above all, the speckless purity of my particular care – the scoured and well-swept floor . . .

EMILY BRONTE
*From "Wuthering Heights."*

I manage the ironing, and keep the rooms clean; Emily does the baking, and attends to the kitchen. We are such odd animals, that we prefer this mode of contrivance to having a new face amongst us. Besides, we do not despair of Tabby's return, and she shall not be supplanted by a stranger in her absence. I excited aunt's wrath very much by burning the clothes, the first time I attempted to iron; but I do better now. Human feelings are queer things; I am much happier black-leading the stoves, making the beds, and sweeping the floors at home, than I should be living like a fine lady anywhere else .

CHARLOTTE BRONTE
*Writing to Ellen Nussey. Tabby had fallen and broken a leg.*

I can hardly tell you how time gets on at Haworth. There is no event whatever to mark its progress. One day resembles another; and all have heavy, lifeless physiognomies. Sunday, baking-day and Saturday are the only ones that have any distinctive mark. Meantime, life wears away. I shall soon be thirty; and I have done nothing yet.

CHARLOTTE BRONTE

I cannot avoid . . . scribbling a few lines to you while I sit here alone, all the household being at church: the sole occupant of an ancient parsonage, among lonely hills . . . After experiencing, since my return home, extreme pain and illness, with mental depression worse than either, I have at length acquired health and strength and soundness of mind, far superior I trust, to anything shown by that miserable wreck you used to know under my name. I can now speak cheerfully and enjoy the company of another without stimulus of six

glasses of whisky; I can write, think and act with some apparent approach to resolution, and I only want a motive for exertion to be happier than I have been for years. But I feel my recovery from almost insanity to be retarded by having nothing to listen to except the wind moaning among old chimneys and older ash trees and nothing to look at except heathery hills walked over when life had all to hope for and nothing to regret with me – no one to speak to except crabbed old Greeks and Romans who have been dust the last five thousand years. And yet this quiet life, from its contrast, makes the year passed at Luddendon Foot appear like a nightmare . . .

BRANWELL BRONTE
*Writing to his friend Grundy.*

We have not been very comfortable here at home latterly. Branwell has, by some means, contrived to get more money from the old quarter, and has led us a sad life . . . Papa is harassed day and night; we have little peace; he is always sick; has two or three times fallen down in fits; what will be the ultimate end, God knows. But who is without their drawback, their scourge, their skeleton behind the curtain? It remains only to do one's best, and endure with patience what God sends.

CHARLOTTE BRONTE
*In a letter dated January 11, 1848.*

An account of one day is an account of all. In the morning, from nine o'clock till half-past twelve, I instruct my sisters, and draw; then we walk till dinner-time. After dinner I sew till tea-time, and after tea I either write, read, or do a little fancy-work, or draw, as I please. Thus, in one delightful, though somewhat monotonous course, my life is passed. I have been only out twice to tea since I came home. We are expecting company this afternoon, and on Tuesday next we shall have all the female teachers of the Sunday-school to tea.

CHARLOTTE BRONTE
*In a letter to Ellen Nussey.*

I got here a little before eight o'clock. All was clean and bright, waiting for me. Papa and the servants were well, and all received me with an affection that should have consoled. The dogs seemed in strange ecstasy. I am certain that they regarded me as the harbinger of others. . . . I felt that the house was all silent, the rooms were all empty. I remembered where the three were laid – in what narrow, dark dwellings – never more to reappear on earth . . . I cannot help thinking of their last days, remembering their sufferings, and what they said and did, and how they looked in mortal affliction . . . To sit in a lonely room, the clock ticking loud through the house.

CHARLOTTE BRONTE

I sometimes think, when late at even,
I climb the stair reluctantly,
Some shape that should be well in heaven
Or ill elsewhere, shall pass me by.

I fear to see the very faces
Familiar thirty years ago,
Even in the old accustomed places,
Which look so cold and gloomy now.

I've come to close the window hither,
At twilight when the sun was down,
And fear my very soul would wither
Lest something should be dimly shown.

Too much the buried form resembling,
Of her who once was mistress here;
Lest doubtful shade, or moonbeam trembling,
Might take her aspect, once so dear.

CHARLOTTE BRONTE

I don't know that I ever saw a spot more exquisitly clean; the most dainty place for that I ever saw. To be sure, the life is like clock-work. No one comes to the house; nothing disturbs the deep repose; hardly a voice is heard; you catch the ticking of the clock in the kitchen, or the buzzing of a fly in the parlour, all over the house. Miss Bronte sits alone in her parlour; breakfasting with her father in his study at nine o'clock. She helps in the housework, for one of their servants, Tabby, is nearly ninety, and the other only a girl. . .

MRS. GASKELL
*Visiting Haworth Parsonage while preparing her biography of*
*Charlotte.*

# Halls and Mansions

Wuthering Heights is the name of Mr. Heathcliff's dwelling. "Wuthering" being a significant provincial adjective, descriptive of the atmospheric tumult to which its station is exposed in stormy weather. Pure, bracing ventilation they must have up there, at all times, indeed; one may guess the power of the north wind, blowing over the edge, by the excessive slant of a few stunted firs at the end of the house, and by a range of gaunt thorns all stretching their limbs one way, as if craving alms of the sun. Happily, the architect had foresight to build it strong; the narrow windows are deeply set in the wall, and the corners defended with large jutting stones.

Before passing the threshold, I paused to admire a quantity of grotesque carvings lavished over the front, and especially about the principal door; above which, among a wilderness of crumbling griffins and shameless little boys, I detected the date "1500" and the name "Hareton Earnshaw" . . . One step brought us into the family sitting-room without any introductory lobby or passage . . . One end reflected splendidly both light and heat from ranks of immense pewter dishes, interspersed with silver jugs and tankards, towering row after row, on a vast oak dresser to the very roof. The latter had never been underdrawn; its entire anatomy lay bare to an inquiring eye, except where a frame of wood laden with oatcakes and clusters of legs of beef, mutton, and ham concealed it. Above the chimney were sundry villainous old guns and a couple of horse-pistols, and, by way of ornament, three gaudily painted canisters disposed along its ledge. The floor was of smooth, white stone; the chairs, high-backed, primitive structures painted green, one or two heavy black ones lurking in the

Opposite: Ponden Hall, Stanbury.

shade. In an arch under the dresser reposed a hugh liver coloured bitch pointer surrounded by a swarm of squealing puppies, and other dogs haunted other recesses.

EMILY BRONTE
*From her novel "Wuthering Heights."*

We ran from the top of the Heights to the park without stopping, Catherine completely beaten in the race, because she was barefoot. You'll have to seek for her shoes in the bog to-morrow. We crept through a broken hedge, groped our way up the path, and planted ourselves on a flower-pot under the drawing-room window. The light came from thence. They had not put up the shutters, and the curtains were only half closed. Both of us were able to look in by standing on the basement and clinging to the ledge, and we saw – ah! it was beautiful – a splendid place carpeted with crimson, and crimson-covered chairs and tables, and a pure white ceiling bordered by gold, a shower of glass-drops hanging in silver chains from the centre, and shimmering with little soft tapers.

EMILY BRONTE
*Thrushcross Grange, from "Wuthering Heights."*

It was three stories high, of proportions not vast, though considerable: a gentleman's manor house, not a nobleman's seat: battlements round the top gave it a picturesque look. It's grey front stood out well from the background of a rookery, whose cawing tenants were now on the wing: they flew over the lawn and grounds to alight in a great meadow, from which these were separated by a sunk fence, and where an array of mighty old thorn trees, strong, knotty, and broad as oaks, at once explained the etymology of the mansion's designation. Farther off were hills; not so lofty as those round Lowood, nor so craggy, nor so like barriers of separation from the living world; but yet quiet and lonely hills enough, and seeming to embrace Thornfield with a seclusion I had not expected to find so near the stirring locality of Millcote.

CHARLOTTE BRONTE
*A first impression of Thornfield in "Jane Eyre."*

In wandering round the shattered walls and through the devastated interior, I gathered evidence that the calamity was not of late occurence. Winter snows, I thought, had drifted through that void arch: winter rains beaten in at those hollow casements; for, amidst the drenched piles of rubbish, spring had cherished vegetation: grass and weed grew here and there between the stones and fallen rafters.

CHARLOTTE BRONTE
*Jane returns to the fire-gutted Thornfield.*

The manor-house of Ferndean was a building of considerable antiquity, moderate size, and no architectural pretensions, deep buried in a wood . . . To this house I came just ere dark on an evening marked by the characteristics of sad sky, cold gale, and continued small, penetrating rain. The last mile I performed on foot . . . When within a very short distance of the manor-house, you could see nothing of it, so thick and dark grew the timber of the gloomy wood about it . . . I thought I had taken a wrong direction and lost my way. The darkness of natural as well as of sylvan dusk gathered over me. I looked round in search of another road. There was none: all was interwoven stem, columnar trunk dense, summer foliage, no opening anywhere, I proceeded: at last my way opened, the trees thinned a little, presently I beheld a railing, then the house –

CHARLOTTE BRONTE
*Writing in "Jane Eyre" of a house which was possibly inspired by Wycoller Hall.*

A few more observations about Horton Lodge and its ongoings, and I have done with dry description for the present. The house was a very respectable one, superior to Mr. Bloomfield's both in age, size, and magnificence. The garden was not so tastefully laid out; but instead of the smooth-shaven lawn, the young trees guarded by palings, the grove of upstart poplars, and the plantation of firs, there was a wide park, stocked with deer, and beautified by fine old trees. The surrounding country itself was pleasant, as far as fertile fields, flourishing trees, quiet green lanes, and smiling hedges with wild flowers scattered along their banks could make it; but it was depressingly flat to one born and nurtured among the rugged hills . . .

ANNE BRONTE
*From "Agnes Grey"*

Wildfell Hall . . . a superannuated mansion of the Elizabethan era, built of dark grey stone, venerable and picturesque to look at, but doubtless cold and gloomy enough to inhabit, with its thick stone mullions and little latticed panes, its time-eaten air-holes, and its too lonely, too unsheltered situation, only shielded from the war of wind and weather by a group of Scots firs, themselves half blighted with storms looking as stern and gloomy as the hall itself.

ANNE BRONTE
*From "The Tenant of Wildfell Hall"*

# Bleak Midwinter

See! how the Winter's howling storms
Burst forth, in all their awful forms,
And hollow frightful sound!
The frost is keen, the wind is high,
The snow falls drifting from the sky,
Fast whitening all around.
The muffled sun withdraws his light,
And leaves the cheerless world, to-night,
And all her gloomy train;
Still louder roars the savage blast,
The frowning shades are thickening fast,
And darker scowls the plain!
Though adverse winds should fiercely blow,
Or heave the breast with sorrow's throe,
Or death stand threatening by;
Blessed is the man and free from harm
O'er whom is stretched His saving arm,
Who peerless reigns on high.

PATRICK BRONTE


The short winter day, as I perceived from the far-declined
sun, was already approaching its close; a chill frost-mist was
rising from the river on which X—— stands, and along whose
banks the road I had taken lay; it dimmed the earth, but did
not obscure the clear icy blue of the January sky.

CHARLOTTE BRONTE
*From "The Professor" in 1853*

Opposite: At Haworth.

The mill-windows were alight, the bell rung loud, and now the little children came running in, in too great a hurry, let us hope, to feel very much nipped by the inclement air; and, indeed, by contrast, perhaps the morning appeared rather favourable to them than otherwise; for they had often come to their work in winter, through snow-storms, through heavy rain, through hard frost.

CHARLOTTE BRONTE
*From "Shirley"*

It was now the middle of the month of February; by six
o'clock therefore, dawn was just beginning to steal on night,
to penetrate with a pale ray its brown obscurity, and give a
demi-translucency to its opaque shadows. Pale enough that
ray was on this particular morning; no colour tinged the east,
no flush warmed it. To see what a heavy lid slowly lifted, what
a wan glance she flung along the hills, you would have thought
the sun's fire quenched last night's floods. The breath of the
morning was chill as its aspect; a raw wind stirred the mass of
night-cloud, and showed, as it slowly rose – leaving a colour-
less, silver-gleaming ring all round the horizon – not blue sky,
but a stratum of paler vapour beyond. It had ceased to rain,
but the earth was sodden, and the pools and rivulets were full.

CHARLOTTE BRONTE
*From "Shirley"*


Silent is the house; all are laid asleep:
One alone looks out o'er the snow-wreaths deep.
Watching every cloud, dreading every breeze
That whirls the wildering drift, and bends the groaning trees.

Cheerful is the hearth, soft the matted floor;
Not one shivering gust creeps through pane or door;
The little lamp burns straight, its rays shoot strong and far;
I trim it well, to be the wanderer's guiding-star.

Burn, then, little lamp; glimmer straight and clear –
Hush! a rustling wind stirs, methinks, the air:
He for whom I wait, thus ever comes to me;
Strange Power! I trust thy might; trust thou my constancy.

EMILY BRONTE

I intended to have written a line yesterday, but just as I was sitting down for the purpose, Arthur called to me to take a walk. We set off, not intending to go far; but though wild and cloudy, it was fine in the morning; when we had got about half-a-mile on the moors, Arthur suggested the idea of the waterfall; after the melted snow, he said it would be fine. I had often wished to see it in its winter power, so we walked on. It was fine indeed; a perfect torrent racing over the rocks, white and beautiful! It began to rain while we were watching it, and we returned home under a streaming sky. However, I enjoyed the walk inexpressibly, and would not have missed the spectacle on any account.

CHARLOTTE BRONTE
*Writing to a friend on November 19, 1854. It was to be her last visit to a favourite waterfall.*

The night is darkening around me,
The wild wind coldly blows;
But a tyrant spell has bound me,
And I cannot, cannot go.

Clouds beyond clouds above me,
Wastes beyond wastes below,
But nothing drear can move me:
I will not, cannot go.

The giant trees are bending
Their bare boughs weighed with snow;
The storm is fast descending,
And yet I cannot go.

EMILY BRONTE
*A poem written when she was 18 years old.*

During January, February, and part of March, the deep snows and, after their melting, the almost impassable roads, prevented our stirring beyond the garden walls, except to go to church; but within these limits we had to pass an hour every day in the open air. Our clothing was insufficient to protect us from the severe cold; we had no boots, the snow got into our shoes and melted there; our ungloved hands became numbed and covered with chilblains; as were our feet: I remember well the distracting irritation I endured from this cause every evening, when my feet inflamed; and the torture of trusting the swelled, raw, and stiff toes into my shoes in the morning. Then the scanty supply of food was distressing; with the keen appetites of growing children, we had scarcely sufficient to keep alive a delicate invalid.

CHARLOTTE BRONTE
*Describing life at Lowood in "Jane Eyre"*


Spring drew on, she was indeed already come; the frosts of winter had ceased; its snows were melted, its cutting winds ameliorated . . . the nights and mornings no longer by their Canadian temperature froze the very blood in our veins; we could now endure the play-hour in the garden: sometimes on a sunny day it began even to be pleasant and genial, and a greenness grew over those brown beds, which, freshening daily, suggested the thought that Hope traversed them at night, and left each morning brighter traces of her steps. Flowers peeped out amongst the leaves: snowdrops, crocuses, purple auricula, and golden-eyed pansies. On Thursday afternoons (half-holidays) we now took walks, and found still sweeter flowers opening by the wayside, under the hedges.

CHARLOTTE BRONTE
*From "Jane Eyre"*

# Wind and Rain

The heavens over the moor were blackening fast. I heard muttering of distant thunder, and saw the frequent flashing of the lightning. Though, ten minutes before, there was scarcely a breath of air stirring, the gale freshened rapidly, and carried along with it clouds of dust and stubble; and by this time some large drops of rain clearly announced an approaching heavy shower. My little family had escaped to a place of shelter, but I did not know it. I consequently watched every movement of the coming tempest with a painful degree of interest. The house was painfully still. Under these circumstances I heard a deep, distant explosion, something resembling, yet something differing from thunder, and I perceived a gentle tremour in the chamber in which I was standing, and in the glass of the window just before me, which, at the time, made an extraordinary impression on my mind; and which, I have no manner of doubt now, was the effect of an Earthquake at the place of eruption. This was a solemn visitation of Providence, which, by the help of God, I shall endeavour to improve.

PATRICK BRONTE
*Of a Waterspout on Crow Hill, September, 1824.*


That Friday made the last of our fine days for a month. In the evening the weather broke; the wind shifted from south to north-east, and brought rain first, and then sleet and snow. On the morrow one could hardly imagine that there had been three weeks of summer – the primroses and crocuses were hidden under wintry drifts, the larks were silent, the young leaves of the early trees smitten and blackened. And dreary, and chill, and dismal, that morrow did creep over!

EMILY BRONTE
*From "Wuthering Heights."*


. . . that wind, pouring in impetuous current through the air, sounding wildly, unremittingly from hour to hour, deepening its tone as the night advances, coming not in gusts, but with a rapid gathering stormy swell – that wind I know is heard at this moment far away in the moors of Haworth. Branwell and Emily hear it, and as it sweeps over our house, down the churchyard, and round the old church, they think perhaps of me and Anne.

CHARLOTTE BRONTE
*At school near Dewsbury.*

Now kawing rooks on rapid pinions move,
For their Lov'd home, the safe sequester'd grove;
Far inland scream the frighten'd sea-gulls loud,
High the blue heron sails along the cloud;
The humming bees, sagacious, homewards fly,
The conscious heifer snuffs the tempest nigh:
But, see! the hazy sun has reached the west,
The murmuring trees proclaim the coming blast.
Fast dusty whirlwinds drive along the plain,
The gusty tempest gives the slacken'd rein;
Low bend the trees, the lofty steeples rock,
And firmest fabrics own the sullen shock.
Condensing fast, the blackening clouds o'erspread
The low'ring sky: the frequent lightning red,
With quivering glance, the streaming clouds do sunder,
And rumbles deep, and long, and loud, the thunder!
The tempest gathering from the murky west,
Rests on the peak, and forms a horrid crest.
Down pour the heavy clouds their copious streams,
Quick shoots the lightning's fiercely vivid gleams;
And loud and louder peals the crashing thunder;
The mountains shake as they would rend asunder . . .

PATRICK BRONTE

The rainy night had ushered in a misty morning, half frost,
half drizzle, and temporary brooks crossed our path, gurgling
from the uplands. My feet were thoroughly wetted. I was
cross and low – exactly the humour suited for making the most
of these disagreeable things.

EMILY BRONTE
*From "Wuthering Heights."*

Though bleak these woods, and damp the ground,
With fallen leaves so thickly strewn,
And cold the wind that wanders round
With wild and melancholy moan;

There is a friendly roof, I know,
Might shield me from the wintry blast;
There is a fire, whose ruddy glow
Will cheer me for my wanderings past.

And so, though still where'er I go
Cold stranger-glances meet my eye;
Though, when my spirit sinks in woe,
Unheeded swells the unbidden sigh.

ANNE BRONTE

About midnight, while we still sat up, the storm came rattling over the Heights in full fury. There was a violent wind, as well as thunder, and either one or the other split a tree off at the corner of the building; a huge bough fell across the roof, and knocked down a portion of the east chimney stack, sending a clatter of stones and soot into the kitchen fire. We thought a bolt had fallen in the middle of us, and Joseph swung on his knees, beseeching the Lord to remember the patriarchs Noah and Lot, and, as in former times, spare the righteous, though He smote the ungodly. I felt some sentiment that it must be a judgement on us also.

EMILY BRONTE
*From "Wuthering Heights."*

One night a thunderstorm broke; a sort of hurricane shook us in our beds; . . . the tempest took hold of me with tyranny; I was roughly roused . . . I got up and dressed myself, and creeping outside the casement close to my bed, sat on its ledge, with my feet on the roof of a lower adjoining building. It was wet, it was wild, it was pitch-dark . . . I could not go in: too restless was the delight of staying with wild hour, black and full of thunder, pealing out such an ode as language never delivered to man – too terribly glorious the spectacle of clouds, split and pierced by white blinding bolts.

CHARLOTTE BRONTE


How different this scene looked when I viewed it laid out beneath the iron sky of winter, stiffened in frost, shrouded with snow! – when mists as chill as death wandered to the impulse of east winds along those purple peaks, and rolled down "ing" and holm till they blended with the frozen fog of the beck! That beck itself was then a torrent, turbid and curbless; it tore asunder the wood, and sent a raving sound through the air, often thickened with wild rain or whirling sleet . . .

CHARLOTTE BRONTE
*From "Jane Eyre"*


The strong blast and the soft breeze; the rough and the halcyon days; the hours of sunrise and sunset; the moonlight and the clouded night, developed for me, in these regions, the same attraction as for them – wound round my faculties the same spell that entranced theirs.

CHARLOTTE BRONTE
*Writing in "Jane Eyre"*

# Summer Days

"One time, however, we were near quarrelling. He said the pleasantest manner of spending a hot July day was lying from morning till evening on a bank of heath in the middle of the moors, with the bees humming dreamily about among the bloom, and the larks singing high up overhead, and the blue sky and bright sun shining steadily and cloudlessly. That was his most perfect idea of heaven's happiness. Mine was rocking in a rustling green tree, with a west wind blowing, and bright white clouds flitting rapidly above, and not only larks, but throstles, and blackbirds, and linnets, and cuckoos pouring out music on every side, and the moors seen at a distance, broken into cool, dusky dells, but close by great swells of long grass undulating in waves to the breeze, and woods and sounding water, and the whole world awake and wild with joy. He wanted all to lie in an estasy of peace; I wanted all to sparkle and dance in a glorious jubilee. I said his heaven would be only half alive, and he said mine would be drunk; I said I should fall asleep in his, and he said he could not breathe in mine, and began to grow very snappish. At last we agreed to try both, as soon as the right weather came; and then we kissed each other and were friends.

EMILY BRONTE
*From "Wuthering Heights"*

I gazed round for a means of diverting her thoughts. On one side of the road rose a high, rough bank, where hazels and stunted oaks, with their roots half exposed, held uncertain tenure. The soil was too loose for the latter, and strong winds had blown some nearly horizontal. In summer, Miss

Opposite: The Worth Valley
at Stanbury.

Catherine delighted to climb along these trunks, and sit in the branches, swinging twenty feet above the ground; and I, pleased with her agility and her light, childish heart, still considered it proper to scold every time I caught her at such an elevation, but so that she knew there was no necessity for descending. From dinner to tea she would lie in her breeze-rocked cradle, doing nothing except singing old songs – my nursery lore – to herself, watching the birds, joint tenants, feed and entice their young ones to fly; or nestling with closed lids, half thinking, half dreaming, happier than words can express.

EMILY BRONTE
*"Wuthering Heights"*

Alone I sat; the summer day
Had died in smiling light away;
I saw it die, I watched it fade
From misty hill and breezeless glade;

EMILY BRONTE
*The first verse of a poem written when she was 19 years old*

It was a mild spring morning, rather soft underfoot, for the last fall of snow was only just wasted away leaving yet a thin ridge here and there lingering on the fresh green beneath the hedges; but beside them already the young primroses were peeping from among the moist dark foliage, and the lark above them singing of summer and hope and love and every heavenly thing.

ANNE BRONTE
*From "The Tenant of Wildfell Hall."*

The grey church looked greyer, and the lonely churchyard lonelier. I distinguished a moor sheep cropping the short turf on the graves. It was sweet, warm weather – too warm for travelling; but the heat did not hinder me from enjoying the delightful scenery above and below. Had I seen it nearer August I'm sure it would have tempted me to waste a month among its solitudes. In winter nothing more dreary, in summer nothing more divine, than those glens shut in by hills, and those bluff, bold swells of heath.

I watched the moths fluttering among the heaths and harebells, listened to the soft wind breathing through the grass, and wondered how anyone could ever imagine unquiet slumbers for the sleep in that quiet earth.

EMILY BRONTE
*From "Wuthering Heights".*

A splendid Midsummer shone over England: skies so pure, suns so radiant as were then seen in long succession, seldom favour, even singly, our wave girt land. It was as if a band of Italian days had come from the South, like a flock of glorious passenger birds, and lighted to rest them on the cliffs of Albion. The hay was all got in; the fields round Thornfield

were green and shorn; the roads white and baked; the trees were in their dark prime; hedge and wood, full-leaved and deeply tinted, contrasted well with the sunny hue of the clear meadows between.

CHARLOTTE BRONTE
*From "Jane Eyre"*

I was not surprised, when I ran down into the hall, to see that a brilliant June morning had succeeded to the tempest of the night; and to feel, through the open glass door, the breathing of a fresh and fragrant breeze. Nature must be gladsome when I was so happy. A beggar-woman and her little boy – pale, ragged objects both – were coming up the walk, and I ran down and gave them all the money I happened to have in my purse – some three or four shillings: good or bad, they must partake my jubilee. The rooks cawed, and blither birds sang; but nothing was so merry or so musical as my own rejoicing heart.

CHARLOTTE BRONTE
*From "Jane Eyre"*

I touched the heath; it was dry, and yet warm with the heat of the summer-day. I looked at the sky; it was pure: a kindly star twinkled just above the chasm ridge. The dew fell, but with propitious softness; no breeze whispered. Nature seemed to me benign and good; I thought she loved me, outcast as I was; and I, who from man could anticipate only mistrust, rejection, insult, clung to her with filial fondness. To-night, at least, I would be her guest – as I was her child: my mother would lodge me without money and without price.

CHARLOTTE BRONTE
*Jane Eyre spends a night out of doors.*

HAWORTH OLD CHURCH.

# Off to Church

Sundays were dreary days in that wintry season. We had to walk two miles to Brocklebridge Church, where our patron officiated. We set out cold, we arrived at church colder; during the morning service we became almost paralysed. It was too far to return for dinner, and an allowance of cold meat and bread, in the same penurious proportion observed in our ordinary meals, was served round between the services. At the close of the afternoon service we returned by an exposed and hilly road, where the bitter winter wind, blowing over a range of snowy summits to the north, almost flayed the skin from our faces.

CHARLOTTE BRONTE
*From "Jane Eyre"*

Gimmerton chapel bells were still ringing; and the full mellow flow of the beck in the valley came soothingly on the ear. It was a sweet substitute for the yet absent murmur of the summer foliage, which drowned the music about the Grange when the trees were in leaf. At Wuthering Heights it always sounded on quiet days, following a great thaw or a season of steady rain . . .

We came to the chapel. I have passed it really in my walks twice or thrice. It lies in a hollow between two hills – an elevated hollow, near a swamp, whose peaty moisture is said to answer all the purposes of embalming, on the few corpses deposited there. The roof has been kept whole hitherto; but as the clergyman's stipend is only twenty pounds per annum, and a house with two rooms, threatening speedily to determine into one, no clergyman will undertake the duties of pastor, especially as it is currently reported that his flock would rather let him starve than increase the living by one penny from their own pockets.

EMILY BRONTE
*From "Wuthering Heights".*


"Well, my rheumatiz got better – I know not whether wi' going to church or not; but one frosty Sunday I got this cold i' my eyes. Th' inflammation didn't come on all at once like, but bit by bit. But I wasn't going to tell you about my eyes; I was talking about my trouble o' mind. And to tell the truth, Miss Grey, I don't think it was anyways eased by coming to church– nought to speak on, at least. I like got my health better, but that didn't mend my soul. I hearkened and hearkened but it was all like sounding brass and a tinkling cymbal. The sermons I couldn't understand, an' th' prayer-book read such good words an' never be no better for it, and often feel it a sore labour an' a heavy task beside, instead of a blessing and a privilege as all good Christians does. It seemed like as all were barren an' dark to me. And then them dreadful words, 'Many shall seek to enter in, and shall not be able.' They like as they fair dried up my sperrit."

ANNE BRONTE
*From "Agnes Grey."*

Mr. Hatfield would come sailing up the aisle, or rather sweeping along like a whirlwind, with his rich silk gown flying behind him, and rustling against the pew doors, mount the pulpit like a conqueror ascending his triumphal car; then sinking on the velvet cushion in an attitude of studied grace, remain in silent prostration for a certain time, then mutter over a Collect and gabble through the Lord's Prayer, rise, draw off one bright lavender glove to give the congregation the benefit of his sparkling rings, lightly pass his fingers through his well-curled hair, flourish a cambric handkerchief, recite a very short passage, or perhaps a mere phrase of Scripture, as a headpiece to his discourse, and finally deliver – a composition.

ANNE BRONTE
*From "Agnes Grey."*

The old church tower and garden wall
Are black with autumn rain,
And dreary winds foreboding call
The darkness down again.

EMILY BRONTE

We allus speak our minds i' this country; and them young
parsons and grand folk fro' London is shocked at were 'incivil-
ity', and we like weel enough to gi'e 'em summat to be
shocked at, 'cause it's sport to us to watch 'em turn up the
whites o' their een, and spreed out their bits o' hands, like as
they're flayed wi' bogards, and then to hear 'em say, nipping
off their words short like – 'Dear! dear! Whet seveges! How
very coarse!'

CHARLOTTE BRONTE
*From "Shirley."*

We had two Sermons on dissent, and its consequences,
preached last Sunday – one in the afternoon by Mr. W., and
one in the evening by Mr. C. All the Dissenters were invited
to come and hear, and they actually shut up their chapels, and
came in a body; of course the church was crowded. Mr. W.
delivered a noble, eloquent, High-Church, Apostolic-
Succession discourse, in which he banged the Dissenters most
fearlessly and unflinchingly. I thought they had got enough for
one while, but it was nothing to the dose that was thrust down
their throats in the evening. A keener, cleverer, bolder, and
more heart-stirring harangue than that Mr. C. delivered from
Haworth pulpit, last Sunday evening, I never heard. He did
not rant; he did not cant; he did not whine; he did not snuggle;
he just got up and spoke with the boldness of a man who was
impressed with the truth of what he was saying, who had no
fear of his enemies, and no dread of consequences. His sermon lasted an hour, yet I was sorry when it was done . . . My

*continued on page 57*

*The giant trees are bending
Their bare boughs weighed
with snow . . .*

EMILY BRONTË

*The frost is keen, the
wind is high,
The snow falls drifting
from the sky*

PATRICK BRONTË

The stone of the
house was of the
same melancholy
tint as the flags of
the walk . . .

FRANK PEEL

*The old church tower and
garden wall
Are black with autumn
rain.*

EMILY BRONTË

*And deepening still the
dream-like charm
Wild moor-sheep feeding
everywhere*

EMILY BRONTË

*Various folks are beginning
to come boring to
Haworth . . . but our rude
hills will form a sufficient
barrier to the frequent
repetition of such visits.*

CHARLOTTE BRONTË

*The Black Bull stands invitingly on the hill-top; while I ate, the hostess talked about the Brontës . . .*

WALTER WHITE

*I fear to see the very faces*
*Familiar thirty years ago,*
*Even in the old accustomed places,*
*Which look so cold and gloomy now.*

CHARLOTTE BRONTË

conscience will not let me be either a Puseyite or a Hookist...
if I were a Dissenter, I would have taken the first opportunity
of kicking or of horse-whipping both the gentlemen for their
stern, bitter attack on my religion and its teachers. But in spite
of all this, I admired the noble integrity which could dictate so
fearless an opposition against so strong an antagonist.

CHARLOTTE BRONTE


We entered the quiet and humble temple; the priest waited in
his white surplice at the lowly altar, the clerk beside him. All
was still; two shadows only moved in a remote corner. My
conjecture had been correct; the strangers had slipped in
before us, and they now stood by the vault of the Rochesters,
their backs towards us, viewing through the rails the old
time-stained marble tomb, where a kneeling angel guarded
the remains of Damer de Rochester, slain at Marston Moor in
the time of the civil wars; and of Elizabeth, his wife.

CHARLOTTE BRONTE
*At the start of the first wedding ceremony in "Jane Eyre."*


Reader, I married him. A quiet wedding we had: he and I, the
parson and clerk, were alone present. When we got back from
church, I went into the kitchen of the manor-house, where
Mary was cooking the dinner, and John cleaning the knives,
and I said:—"Mary, I have been married to Mr. Rochester this
morning." The housekeeper and her husband were both of
that decent phlegmatic order of people, to whom one may at
any time safely communicate a remarkable piece of news
without incurring the danger of having one's ears pierced by
some shrill ejaculation, and subsequently stunned by a torrent of wordy wonderment. Mary did look up, and she did
stare at me: a ladle with which she was basting a pair of

chickens roasting at the fire, did for some three minutes hang
suspended in the air; and for the same space of time John's
knives also had a rest from the polishing process: but Mary,
bending again over the roast, said only – "Have you, Miss?
Well, for sure!"

CHARLOTTE BRONTE
*From "Jane Eyre."*

*From a photograph made about 1867*

# Conversation Pieces

When he next spoke, it was in a less querulous tone, to ask what there was for dinner.

"Turkey and grouse", was the concise reply.

"And what besides?"

"Fish".

"What kind of fish?"

"I don't know."

*"You don't know?"* cried he, looking solemnly up from his plate, and suspending his knife and fork in astonishment.

"No. I told the cook to get some fish; I did not particularise what."

"Well, that beats everything! A lady professes to keep house, and doesn't even know what fish for dinner! professes to order fish, and doesn't specify what!"

"Perhaps, Mr. Bloomfield, you will order dinner yourself in future."

ANNE BRONTE
*From "Agnes Grey"*

"Well, Miss Matilda is quite as good – better, in one respect."

"What is that?"

"She's honest."

"And the other is not?"

"I should not call her *dis*honest; but it must be confessed she's a little artful."

ANNE BRONTE
*From "Agnes Grey"*

"Were you asked to tea?" she demanded, tying an apron over her neat black frock, and standing with a spoonful of leaf poised over the pot.

"I shall be glad to have a cup," I answered.

"Were you asked?" she repeated.

"No," I said, half smiling. "You are the proper person to ask me."

She flung the tea back, spoon and all, and resumed her chair . . .

EMILY BRONTE
*"Wuthering Heights"*

"Nelly, do you never dream queer dreams?" she said suddenly, after some minutes reflection.

"Yes; now and then," I answered.

"And so do I. I've dreamt in my life dreams that have stayed with me ever after, and changed my ideas; they've gone through and through me, like wine through water, altered the colour of my mind. And this is one. I'm going to tell it; but take care not to smile at any part of it."

EMILY BRONTE
*"Wuthering Heights"*

The lattice was open, and as he stepped out I heard Cathy inquiring of her unsociable attendant what was that inscription over the door? Hareton stared up, and scratched his head like a true clown.

"It's some damnable writing," he answered. "I cannot read it."

"Can't read it?" cried Catherine. "I can read it; it's English. But I want to know why it is there."

Opposite: Three views
of Haworth

EMILY BRONTE
*"Wuthering Heights"*

"When shall I see you again, Miss Murray?"

"At church, I suppose," replied she, "unless your business chances to bring you here again, at the precise moment when I happen to be walking by."

"I could always manage to have business here, if I knew precisely when and where to find you."

"But if I would, I could not inform you, for I am so immethodical, I never can tell to-day what I shall do tomorrow."

ANNE BRONTE
*From "Agnes Grey"*

"Who is in the wrong, then, Lucy?"

"Me, Dr. John – me; and a great abstraction on whose wide shoulders I like to lay the mountains of blame they were sculptured to bear – me and Fate."

"Me' must take better care in future," said Dr. John, smiling, I suppose, at my bad grammar.

CHARLOTTE BRONTE
*From "Villette"*

"But papa!"

"Well?"

"I see an obstacle."

"I don't at all."

"It is enormous, papa; it can never be got over. It is as large as you in your greatcoat, and the snowdrift on the top."

"And, like that snowdrift, capable of melting?"

CHARLOTTE BRONTE
*From "Villette"*

"What does 'a bit wildish' mean?" I inquired.

"It means destitute of principle, and prone to every vice that is common to youth."

"But I've heard uncle say he was a sad wild fellow himself when he was young."

She sternly shook her head.

"He was jesting, then, I suppose," said I.

ANNE BRONTE
*From "The Tenant of Wildfell Hall"*

"Do you always brush your hat so carefully, and do your hair so nicely, and put on such smart new gloves when you take a walk?"

"Not always."

"You're going to Wildfell Hall, aren't you?"

"What makes you think so?"

"Because you look as if you were; but I wish you wouldn't go so often."

ANNE BRONTE
*From "The Tenant of Wildfell Hall"*

"This world is an absurd one," said he.

"Why so, Mr. Hunsden?"

"I wonder you should ask. You are yourself a strong proof of the absurdity I allude to."

CHARLOTTE BRONTE
*From "The Professor"*

# Into Print

"Entered school August 10, 1824. Writes indifferently, Ciphers a little, and works neatly. Knows nothing of grammar, geography, history or accomplishments. Altogether clever of her age, but knows nothing systematically. Left school June 1, 1825."

ABOUT CHARLOTTE
*From the records of Cowan Bridge School.*

I accidentally lighted on a M.S. volume of verse in my sister Emily's handwriting. Of course I was not surprised, knowing that she could and did write verse. I looked it over, and something more than suprise seized me – a deep conviction that these were not common effusions, not at all like the poetry women generally write. I thought them condensed and terse, vigorous and genuine. To my ear they had also peculiar music, wild, melancholy and elevating. My sister Emily was not a demonstrative character, nor one on the recesses of whose mind and feelings even those nearest and dearest to her could, with impunity, intrude unlicensed; it took hours to reconcile her to the discovery I had made, and days to persuade her that such poems merited publication.

CHARLOTTE BRONTE
*In the autumn of 1845.*

We had very early cherished the dream of one day becoming authors. This dream, never relinquished even when distance divided and absorbing tasks occupied us, now suddenly acquired strength and consistency; *it took the character of a resolve.*

CHARLOTTE BRONTE
*Writing in 1845.*

Our book is found to be a drug; no man needs it or heeds it. In the space of a year our publisher has disposed of but of two copies, and by what painful efforts he succeeded in getting rid of these two, himself only knows.

CHARLOTTE BRONTE
*Writing about the sisters' book of poems, 1847.*

I have, since I saw you at Halifax, devoted my hours of time snatched from downright illness, to the composition of a three-volume *Novel* – one volume of which is completed – and along with the two forthcoming ones, has been really the result of half a dozen by-past years of thoughts about, and experience in, this crooked path of Life . . . Noble writings, works of art, music or poetry now instead of rousing my imagination, cause a whirlwind of blighting sorrow that sweeps over my mind with unspeakable dreariness, and if I sit down and try to write, all ideas that used to come clothed in sunlight now press round me in funeral black . . . I shall never be able to realise the too sanguine hopes of my friends, for at 28 I am a thoroughly *old man.*

BRANWELL BRONTE
*Writing to his friend Leyland.*

Permit me, Sir, to caution you against forming too favourable an idea of my powers, or too sanguine an expectation of what they can achieve. I am, myself, sensible both of deficiencies of capacity and disadvantages of circumstance: which will, I hear, render it somewhat difficult for me to attain popularity as an author . . . Still, if health be spared and time vouchsafed me, I mean to do my best.

CHARLOTTE BRONTE
*To the publisher who had just accepted "Jane Eyre."*

The six copies of "Jane Eyre" reached me this morning. You have given the work every advantage which good paper, clear type, and a seemly outside can supply:– if it fails, the fault will lie with the author – you are exempt. I now await the judgement of the press and the public.

CHARLOTTE BRONTE
*Acknowledging a letter from Smith, Elder and Company, 1847.*

If I ever *do* write another book, I think I will have nothing of what you call "melodrama"; I think so, but I am not sure. I *think*, too, I will endeavour to follow the counsel which shines out of Miss Austin's "mild eyes", "to finish more and more subdued"; but neither am I sure of that. When authors write best, or, at least, when they write most fluently, an influence seems to waken in them, which becomes their master – which will have its own way – putting out of view all behests but its own, dictating certain words, and insisting on their being used, whether vehement or measured in their nature; new moulding characters, giving unthought of turns to incidents, rejecting carefully-elaborated old ideas, and suddenly creating and adopting new ones. Is it not so? And should we try to counteract this influence? Can we indeed counteract it?

CHARLOTTE BRONTE
*To G. H. Lewis, who wrote about "Jane Eyre" in the "Frazer" magazine.*

She informed me that something like the following conversation took place between her and him. (I wrote down her words the day after I heard them; and I am pretty sure they are quite accurate).

"Papa, I've been writing a book."

"Have you my dear?"

"Yes, and I want you to read it."

"I am afraid it will try my eyes too much."

"But it is not in manuscript; it is printed."

"My dear! you've never thought of the expense it will be! It will be almost sure to be a loss, for how can you get a book sold? No one knows you or your name."

"But papa, I don't think it will be a loss; no more will you, if you will just let me read you a review or two, and tell you more about it."

So she sat down and read some of the reviews to her father;

and then, giving him the copy of "Jane Eyre" that she intended for him, she left him to read it. When he came into tea, he said: "Girls, do you know Charlotte has been writing a book, and it is much better than likely?"

ELIZABETH GASKELL
*Reporting a story related by Charlotte.*

This is the first work published by my daughter, under the fictitious name of "Currer Bell", which is the usual way at first by authors, but her real name is everywhere known. She sold the copyright of this and her other two works for fifteen hundred pounds, so that she has to pay for the books she gets the same as others. Her other two books are in six volumes. In two years hence, when all shall be published in a cheaper form, if all be well, I may send them. You can let my brothers and sisters read this.

PATRICK BRONTE
*Writing to his brother Hugh in Ireland, 1853*

The announcement of Miss Bronte's authorship was a day that I have heard poeple of Haworth speak of as one of public rejoicings. We will let Miss Bronte narrate how the news fell on her startled ears. "Mr. —— having finished 'Jane Eyre' is now crying out for the other book. Mr. —— has finished 'Shirley', he is delighted with it. John ——'s wife, seriously thought him gone wrong in the head, as she heard him giving vent to roars of laughter as he sat alone, clapping and stamping on the floor. He would read all the scenes about the curates aloud to papa. Martha came in yesterday, puffing and blowing and much excited. "I've heard sich news!" she began. "What about?" "Please, ma'am, you've been and written two books – the grandest books that ever was seen".

*From "Haworth Past and Present."*

# Moments of Sadness

And when my dear wife was dead and buried and gone; and when I missed her at every corner, and when her memory was hourly raised by the innocent yet distressing prattle of my children, I do assure you my dear Sir, from what I felt, I was happy at the recollection that to sorrow, not as those without hope, was no sin; that our Lord himself had wept over his departed friend . . .

PATRICK BRONTE

In my own register of transactions during my nights and days I find no matter worthy of extraction for your Perusal. All is yet with me clouds and darkness. I hope you have at least, blue sky and sunshine. Constant and unavoidable depression of mind and body sadly shackle me in even trying to go on with any mental effort which might rescue me from the fate of a dry toast soaked six hours in a glass of cold water, and intended to be given an old Maid's Squeamish Cat.

BRANWELL BRONTE
*Writing to F. A. Leyland*

The past three weeks have been a dark interval in our humble home. Branwell's constitution had been failing fast all the summer; but still neither the doctors nor himself thought him so near his end as he was. He was entirely confined to his bed but for one single day, and was in the village two days before his death. He died, after 20 minutes struggle, on Sunday morning, September 24th. He was perfectly conscious till the last agony came on. His mind had undergone the peculiar change which frequently preceeds death, two day previously; the calm of better feelings filled it; a return of natural affection marked his last moments.

CHARLOTTE BRONTE
*On the death of Branwell*

Never in all her life had she lingered over any tasks that lay before her, and she dare not now. "She sank rapidly, she made haste to leave us. Day by day, when I saw with what a front she met suffering, I looked on her with an anguish of wonder and love. I have seen nothing like it; but, indeed, I have never seen her parallel in anything. Stronger than a man, simpler than a child, her nature stood alone. The awful point was that, while full of love for others, for herself she had no pity; the spirit was inexorable to the flesh; from the trembling hand, the unnerved limbs, the fading eyes, the same service was exacted as they had rendered in health. To stand by and witness this, and not dare to remonstrate, was a pain no words can render. She made no complaint; she would not endure questioning; she rejected sympathy and help.

CHARLOTTE BRONTE
*On the death of Emily*

We often pity the poor because they have no leisure to mourn their departed relatives, and necessity obliges them to labour through their severest afflictions; but is not active employ-ment the best remedy for overwhelming sorrow, the surest antidote for despair? It may be a rough comforter, it may seem hard to be harassed with the cares of life when we have no relish for its enjoyments, to be goaded to labour when the heart is ready to break, and the vexed spirit implores for rest only to weep in silence; but is not labour better than the rest we covet? and are not those petty, tormenting cares less hurtful than a continual brooding over the great affliction that oppresses us? Besides, we cannot have cares, and anxieties, and toil, without hope – if it be but the hope of fulfilling our joyless task, accomplishing some needful project, or escaping some further annoyance.

ANNE BRONTE
*From "Agnes Grey"*

I love the silent hour of night,
For blissful dreams may then arise,
Revealing to my charmed sight
What may not bless my waking eyes.

And then a voice may meet my ear
That death has silenced long ago;
And hope and rapture may appear
Instead of solitude and woe.

Cold in the grave for years has lain
The form it was my bliss to see;
And only dreams can bring again
The darling of my heart to me.

ANNE BRONTE
*A poem entitled "Night" (1844)*


She died very calmly and gently: she was quite sensible to the last. About three minutes before she died, she said she was very happy, and believed she was passing out of earth into heaven. It was not her custom to talk much about religion; but she was very good, and I am certain she is now in a far better place than any this world contains.

CHARLOTTE BRONTE
*On the death of Anne*


I thank you for your kind sympathy. My daughter is indeed dead, and the solemn truth presses upon her worthy and affectionate husband and me, with great, it may be with unusual weight. But others also have or shall have their sorrows, and we feel our own the most. The marriage that took place seem'd to hold forth long and bright prospects of happiness, but in the inscrutable providence of God, all our hopes have ended in disappointment and our joy in the mourning. May we resign to the Will of the Most High. After three months of sickness, tranquil death closed the scene. But our loss we trust is her gain. But why should I trouble you longer with our sorrows? The heart knoweth its own bitterness – and we ought to bear with fortitude our own grievances and not to bring others into our sufferings . . . .

PATRICK BRONTE
*Writing to Mrs. Gaskell following the death of Charlotte, on*
*April 5, 1855*

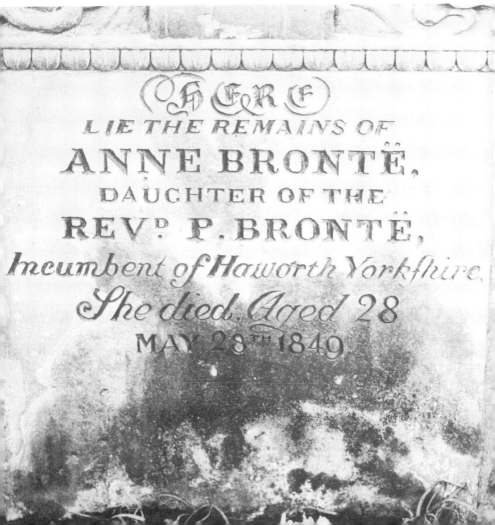

# Birds and Beasts

Some time passed before I felt tranquil even here: I had a vague dread that wild cattle might be near, or that some sportsman or poacher might discover me. If a gust of wind swept the waste, I looked up, fearing it was the rush of a bull; if a plover whistled, I imagined it a man. Finding my apprehensions unfounded, however, and calmed by the deep silence that reigned as evening declined at nightfall, I took confidence . . .

At last the woods rose; the rookery clustered dark; a loud cawing broke the morning stillness. Strange delight inspired me: on I hastened. Another field crossed – a lane threaded – and there were the courtyard walls – the back offices: the house itself, the rookery still hid. "My first view of it shall be in front," I determined, "where its bold battlements will strike the eye nobly at once, and where I can single out my master's very window . . . ." The crows sailing overhead perhaps watched me while I took this survey. I wonder what they thought: they must have considered I was very careful and timid at first, and that gradually I grew very bold and reckless.

And now I can recall the picture of the grey old house of God rising calm before me, of a rook wheeling round the steeple, of a ruddy morning sky beyond.

CHARLOTTE BRONTE
*From "Jane Eyre"*

Opposite: Young curlews
at a moorland nest.

The linnet in the rocky dells;
The moor-lark in the air,
The bee among the heather-bells
That hide my lady fair.

'It was spring, for the skylark was singing.'
Those words, they awakened a spell –
They unlocked a deep fountain whose springing
Nor Absence nor Distance can quell.

EMILY BRONTE


We have got Flossy; got and lost Tiger; lost the hawk Hero,
which with the geese, was given away, and is doubtless dead, for
when I came back from Brussels, I inquired on all hands and
could hear nothing of him. Tiger died early last year. Keeper
and Flossy are well, also the canary acquired four years since.
We are now all at home, and likely to be there some time.

EMILY BRONTE
*From her Diary, July 30th, 1845*

The mute bird sitting on the stone,
The dank moss dripping from the wall,
The thorn-trees gaunt, the walks o'ergrown,
I love them, how I love them all!

EMILY BRONTE


Presently I heard a snuffling sound behind me, and then a dog
came frisking and wriggling to my feet. It was my own Snap –
the little, dark, wire-haired terrier! When I spoke his name he
leapt up in my face and yelled for joy. Almost as much
delighted as himself, I caught the little creature in my arms,
and kissed him repeatedly. But how came he to be there? He
could not have dropped from the sky or come all that way

alone. It must be either his master, the rat-catcher, or some-body else that had brought him. So, repressing my extravag-ant caresses, and endeavouring to repress his likewise, I looked round, and beheld – Mr Weston!

ANNE BRONTE
*From "Agnes Grey"*

"Mary, mamma says I'm to help you, or get you to take a walk with me. She says you may well look thin and dejected if you sit so constantly in the house."

"Help me you cannot, Agnes; and I cannot go out with *you*. I have far too much to do."

"Then let me help you."

"You cannot, indeed, dear child. Go and practise your music, or play with the kitten" . . . It was time enough for me to sit bending over my work, like a grave matron, when my favourite little pussy was become a steady old cat.

ANNE BRONTE
*From "Agnes Grey"*

Emily Jane Bronte M. ay the 29 1829

1802. – This September I was invited to devastate the moors of a friend in the north, and on my journey to his abode I unexpectedly came within fifteen miles of Gimmerton. The ostler at a roadside public-house was holding a pail of water to refresh my horses, when a cart of very green oats, newly reaped, passed by, and he remarked, – "Yon's frough Gimmerton, nah! They're allas three wick after other folk wi' ther harvest."

I departed to renew my search. Its result was disappointment, and Joseph's quest ended in the same.

"Yon lad gets war un war!" observed he on re-entering. "He's left th' yate at t' full swing, and miss's pony has trodden dahn two rigs o' corn, and plottered through, raight o'er into t' meadow! Hhasomdiver, t' maister 'ull play t'devil to-morn, and he'll do weel. He's patience itsself wi' sich careless, offald craters – patience itsseln he is! Bud he'll not be soa allus – Yah's see, all on ye! Yah munn't drive him out of his head for nowt!

EMILY BRONTE
*From "Wuthering Heights"*

Keeper may visit Emily's little bedroom – as he still does day by day – and Flossie may still look wistfully round for Anne, they will never see them again – nor shall I – as least the human part of me.

CHARLOTTE BRONTE

On the 26th she drove on the sands an hour, and lest the poor donkey should be urged to a greater speed than her heart throught right, she took the reins and drove herself. When joined by her friend, she was charging the boy – master of the donkey – to treat the animal well. She was ever fond of dumb things, and would relinquish her own comfort for theirs.

ELLEN NUSSEY
*Writing about Anne Bronte*

Sleep, O cluster of friends,
Sleep! or only, when May,
Brought by the West Wind, returns
Back to your native heaths,
And the plover is heard on the moors,
Yearly awake, to behold
The opening summer, the sky,
The shining moorland; to hear
The drowsy bee, as of old,
Hum o'er the thyme, the grouse
Call from the heather in bloom!

Sleep; or only for this
Break your united repose.

MATTHEW ARNOLD
*From "Haworth Churchyard," 1855*

Sweet briar and southernwood, jasmine, pink, and rose, have long been yielding their evening sacrifice of incense: this new scent is neither of shrub nor flower; it is – I know it well – it is Mr. Rochester's cigar. I look round and listen. I see trees laden with ripening fruit. I hear a nightingale, warbling in a wood half a mile off; no moving form is visible, no coming step audible; but that perfume increases: I must flee.

CHARLOTTE BRONTE
*From "Jayne Eyre"*

# Their Living Faith

NO COWARD SOUL IS MINE,
No trembler in the world's storm-troubled sphere:
I see Heaven's glories shine,
And Faith shines equal, arming me from Fear.

O God within my breast,
Almighty, ever-present Deity!
Life, that in me has rest
As I, undying Life, have power in Thee!

Vain are the thousand creeds
That move men's hearts; unutterably vain;
Worthless as withered weeds,
Or idlest froth amid the boundless main,

To waken doubt in one
Holding so fast by Thine infinity,
So surely anchored on
The steadfast rock of Immortality.

With wide-embracing love
Thy Spirit animates eternal years,
Pervades and brooks above,
Changes, sustains, dissolves, creates, and rears.

Though earth and man were gone,
And suns and universes ceased to be,
And Thou wert left alone,
Every existence would exist in Thee.

There is not room for Death,
Nor atom that his might could render void:
Thou – Thou art Being and Breath,
And what Thou art may never be destroyed.

EMILY BRONTE

MY SOUL IS AWAKENED, MY SPIRIT IS SOARING
And carried aloft on the wings of the breeze:
For above and around me the wild wind is roaring,
Arousing to rapture the earth and the seas.

The long withered grass in the sunshine is glancing,
The bare trees are tossing their branches on high;
The dead leaves beneath them are merrily dancing,
The white clouds are scudding across the blue sky.

I wish I could see how the ocean is lashing
The foam of its billows to whirlwinds of spray;
I wish I could see how its proud waves are dashing,
And hear the wild roar of their thunder today!

ANNE BRONTE

A Study of Anne Bronte

WE WOVE A WEB IN CHILDHOOD
A web of sunny air;
We dug a spring in infancy
Of water pure and fair;

We sowed in youth a mustard seed
We cut an almond rod;
We are now grown up to riper age –
Are they withered in the sod?

The mustard-seed in distant land
Bends down a mighty tree,
The dry unbudding almond wand
Has touched eternity . . .

CHARLOTTE BRONTE
*Writing in 1835*

## BELIEVE NOT THOSE WHO SAY

The upward path is smooth
Lest thou shouldst stumble in the way,
And faint before the truth.

It is the only road
Unto the realms of joy;
But he who seeks that blest abode
Must all his powers employ.

Bright hopes and pure delights
Upon his course may beam,
And there; amidst the sternest heights,
The sweetest flowerets gleam.

On all her breezes borne,
Earth yields no scents like those;
But he that dares not grasp the thorn
Should never crave the rose.

Arm – arm thee for the fight!
Cast useless loads away;
Watch through the darkest hours of night.
Toil through the hottest day.

Crush pride into the dust,
Or thou must needs be slack;
And trample down rebellious lust,
Or it will hold thee back.

Seek not thy honour here;
Waive pleasures and renown;
The world's dread scoff undaunted bear,
And face its deadliest frown.

To labour and to love,
To pardon and endure,
To lift thy heart to God above,
And keep thy conscience pure;

Be this thy constant aim,
Thy hope, thy chief delight;
What matter who should whisper blame,
Or who should scorn or slight?

If but thy God approve,
And if, within they breast,
Thou feel the comfort of His Love,
The earnest of His Rest.

ANNE BRONTE
*April, 1848*


## I HOPED THAT WITH THE BRAVE AND STRONG

My portioned task might lie;
To toil among the busy throng,
With purpose pure and high;
But God has fixed another part,

And He has fixed it well;
I said so with my bleeding heart,
When first the anguish fell.

Thou God has taken our delight,
Our treasured hope away;
Thou bid'st us now weep through the night
And sorrow through the day.

These weary hours will not be lost,
These days of misery,
These nights of darkness, tempest tossed,
Can I but turn to Thee?

If Thou should being me back to life,
More humble I should be;
More wise – more strengthened for the strife –
More apt to lean on Thee;
Should death be standing at the gate
Thus should I keep vow;
But Lord, whatever be my fate;
Oh, let me serve Thee now.

ANNE BRONTE
*She died at Scarborough in May, 1849*

# A Host of Visitors

Various folks are beginning to come boring to Haworth, on the wise errand of seeing the scenery described in *Jane Eyre* and *Shirley* . . . but our rude hills and rugged neighbourhood will I doubt not form a sufficient barrier to the frequent repetition of such visits . . .

CHARLOTTE BRONTE
*Writing in 1850*

I was shown across the lobby into the parlour to the left, and there I found Miss Bronte, standing in the full light of the window, and I had ample opportunity of fixing her upon my memory, where her image is vividly present to this hour. She was diminutive in height, and extremely fragile in figure. Her hand was one of the smallest I have ever grasped. She had no pretensions to being considered beautiful, and was as far removed from being plain. She had rather light brown hair, somewhat thin, and drawn plainly over her brow. Her complexion had no trace of colour in it, and her lips were pallid also; but she had a most sweet smile, with a touch of tender melancholy in it. Altogether she was as unpretending, undemonstrative, quiet a little lady as you could well meet. Her age I took to be about five-and-thirty. But when you saw and felt her eyes the spirit that created Jane Eyre was revealed at once to you. They were rather small, but of a very peculiar colour, and had a strange lustre and intensity.

JOHN STORES SMITH
*A Mancunian, visiting the Brontes in 1850*

Opposite: Main Street
at Haworth

A low stone house occupied one corner of the graveyard. A field had evidently been set apart, and the founders of the church had said "in three-quarters of it we will enter the dead, and in that other fourth we will bury the living." A little garden was before it, and you stepped straight off the graveyard into it. You also went down one step, as towards a larger grave. A flagged walk led up to the front door, and it was covered over with a damp green film, and in the interstices grew an almost black moss. The stone of the house was of the same melancholy tint as the flags of the walk: of all the sad, heart-broken dwellings I have passed this was the saddest.

FRANK PEEL
*Writing of Haworth Parsonage in 1855*

Keighley has been chiefly made known to us from its proximity to Haworth, Charlotte Bronte's home. When did we ever hear or think of it before? Yet it is one of those inportant and swarming manufacturing places that make the power and wealth of England; and, as I arrived on pay-day afternoon, the streets were thronged with thousands of factory-people, bearing the hard and independent stamp of West Riding weavers, described so vigorously in *Shirley*. In the dull and up-hill ride of four miles to Haworth, shut in most of the way by high stone walls, instead of the usual green hedges, I could not but think of those two feeble sisters, struggling along afoot over this dreary road, in the thunderstorm, on their way to Keighley to take the London train, for the purpose of proving to their publisher their actual and separate identity. We passed several great stone walls that might have been very well used for fortresses.

JAMES M. HOPPIN

Opposite: The Parsonage
at Haworth

The Black Bull stands invitingly on the hill-top. I was ready for breakfast and the hostess quite ready to serve; and while I ate she talked of the family who made Haworth famous. She knew them all, brother and sisters: Mr. Nicholls had preached the day before in the morning; Mr. Bronte in the afternoon. It was mostly in the afternoon that the old gentleman preached, and he delivered his sermon without a book. The people felt sorry for his bereavements; and they all liked Mr. Nicholls.

WALTER WHITE
*From "A Month in Yorkshire" (1858)*

Martha then showed me into the kitchen for a moment. This had been Tabby's kingdom. Everything was exquisitely neat, and the copper pans shone like gold. It was a snug, warm, crooning place; and it was not difficult to see the picture, on a dark winter eve, when the storms howled over the moor and rattled against the windows, of those bright-fancied children crouching together around the fire, telling their strange stories, and living in a world created by themselves. Here Emily Bronte studied German, with her book propped up before her, while she kneaded dough. Now all are gone; and the old father, shutting up many things in his own impene-trable mind, was still living on alone, thinking more perhaps of meeting his children again in a sinless and sorrowless world, than of all their fame in this.

JAMES M. HOPPIN
*Visiting the Parsonage in the 1860s*

Then we walked out on the moor – the favourite walk of all the Brontes. The sexton told me that the moor stretched away nearly 12 miles without interruption of any sort: I supposed this must be an exaggeration, but I find by the reduced ord-nance map that the remark is almost precisely true. Mr

Opposite: Haworth

Bronte used to be seen to walk out to a certain place; stop; look around him gazing; turn on his steps: and return. It is in August that the moor is in its glory – then the heath is in full bloom, a rich purple, extending miles away. Now it was brown and dark.

CHARLES HALE
*An American who visited the Bronte haunts in 1861*

In all the talk of the Brontes however it is very singular how all these people at once diverge from the girls to Branwell, although acknowledging his despicable character, his profligacy and its deplorable incidents and consequences.

CHARLES HALE

Our guide spoke with great affection of Charlotte, who was evidently his favourite of the sisters. "Emily," he said, "was taller and more prepossessing like and less melancholy." Anne he briefly described as "a nice little thing." We looked with deep interest at the tablet containing the long list of names, the poor mother, the six children, and lastly the poor old father after all his bereavements. We had a strongly cherished opinion that the father was a harsh, disagreeable man, but the sexton, in a simple and truly polite way, said: "It is not for me to contradict you, but if you felt as I do, you would speak differently".

EMILY SARAH DAWSON
*A young visitor to Haworth in Autumn, 1866*

Visiting Currer Bell's birthplace and tomb at Haworth, I was struck by the considerable number of admirers who, in the past fifteen years have signed the visitor's book. I counted more than three thousand! . . . Among those names there were many Americans, Germans, Italians and only three Frenchmen! There are four now!

FRANCOIS-ODYSSE BAROT
*In a book published in France, 1874*